THE WILD ROAD TO JOY, PEACE, AND JUSTICE

Poems and Jokes

BY

ZANE H. TREFIELD

DEDICATION:

To the strong people I know who do their best, are kind and strong, but do not always get fair treatment from the world, like CJ Rimple, Aaron Due, and Brock Bartel.

Keep fighting, keep shining, keep smiling. He is near to the broken-hearted. There may be pain for now, but joy is just around the bend.

ACKNOWLEDGEMENTS

To the allies in the Oklahoma comedy scene like Spencer Mills, Kyle Fleming, Joe Eaton, Tyler McCance, Preston Sly, Miranda Chase, Caty Coffee and Nathan, JB Watkins, Aaron Due, Aiden Hgstra, and Grant Schaefer, Kitty Gilligan, Brandon Killough, and Leo Mendez, and Kayvon Taghizadeh—you all have gone alongside me and helped me through storms and seen the mountaintops at times with me. To the remnant support in the Boston scene such as Tyrone Jones (for calling me a legend), Stirling Smith, showing me how to do stand-up workshops (for the comedy walks and showing me how to do a comedy workshop), Lloyd Legacy Sharp (good vibes and the Sponsor Guy), Sam Ike (4 walls and a microphone) and Casey Crawford (humility and kindness)—you all are talented and solid people and I loved getting to learn comedy from you all.

To the family members who encouraged my poetry.

To my church family at Roots Church, especially Pastor Jonathan and Cathleen Gibson. Your support and encouragement are cherished forever. Your example of the body of Christ is a testimony to your love of God and your fellow man.

To Charlie Kip who was a big reason I published my first book. You are a strong leader and intelligent writer. Keep fighting for good.

To the people who have seen me do comedy and supported it. The laughs meant more than you will ever know and without you all, life would be pretty hard and vanilla.

To my Lord and Savior, for propelling me through the darkest seasons, for giving me fresh ideas, for giving me joy that I cannot explain, for saving me and giving me a future.

Praise for Zane H. Trefield's first book, "The Lessons of a Baseball Player Who Dreams of Playing on a Field of Bread."

"Excellent writer with anecdotes about traveling the country along with quips about navigating life in the modern world."-Steven Allen, Tulsa-based comedian

My thought was, "Can this be really happening to him?" You will see the aspirations of a young man, his love for baseball, and his struggles. A refreshing reveal of lessons learned by the author. -Robb Lee, a friend and bus driver

I have met many fair-weather Cowboys fans and friends who only show up during the good times, but Caleb (Zane) has always been a loyal and compassionate friend with an amazing sense of humor during the good, bad, and turbulent times in life.

"One if the greatest gifts anyone can give us is a piece of their real life and wisdom they paid for in blood, sweat, and tears. I know you will laugh, I hope you will think, and I pray you will use Zane's insights to make your own dreams come true and begin living the life you were created to live."-Jim Stovall, Best-Selling Author and Filmmaker

INTRODUCTION

Hello, dear reader,

I just want to take the time to thank you for acquiring this book and taking the time to pick it up and read it. You are in the top 3% of humans. These poems are from the early parts of my writing career and the jokes at the end are a mix from 15-years of doing stand-up comedy. I would love to hear your thoughts on these writings. My phone number is 918-859-9789. We could even share a meal to discuss the book or anything else on your mind. May God bless you and keep you and his face shine upon you, and may he be gracious to you.

Signed,

Zane H. Trefield

P.S. Matthew 10:8—"Freely you have been given so freely give"

MEANING

It feels like one of those days,

Where the weight of my life

Comes to a halting stop.

Maybe it is just a phase.

They say you have one life.

They say get a job,

Nice home, pretty wife.

Is that all there is to it?

They say be tough, have grit.

Don't make waves or drama.

Don't run; you have to sit.

It all makes me weary, thirsty.

Since it's my life and only one,

Here's the deal:

I'm not going to be good

When I know I can be great.

And my life they'll no more steal.

THRIVING IN THE BIG APPLE

With a city with so many a nickname,

You'd think New York is magic

The hype says you'll find fame

The possibilities they list, never tragic.

They say you'll find fun, even a dame.

But is all this accurate or not?

Yes and no is what I have to say.

At first you will be a tiny blot.

If you don't try you'll stay that way.

You must mastermind a grand plot.

You can't just seek friends and fun.

For those kinds remain a tiny spot.

And are easily, repeatedly outdone.

To those wanting more than the status quo

I say, yes, you can go out and see the city,

This city of lights and unstopping glow,

The city that in the movies is always pretty.

Go out and up that famous Empire building,

Go see Central Park and its charm after dark

See the broad shows that don't lack gilding.

See Times Square's irresistible spark

Having fun, don't let yourself be outworked

For in this city with rents through the roof.

You can be way behind and still overworked.

Many here will smile but really be aloof.

But this is what I have to say today:

Here when you rise to the top of the chart,

It's of colossal scale and here to stay.

So, have a good mood and a happy heart

When you've made yourself a success here,

You've done what most didn't, won't start.

For you've become more than a sight-seer.

Those that win here are the smallest group,

For they rose, flew and left the clucking coop.

YOU AND I

All else can be wrong and hard.

With you, though, it's right and easy

Because you are who you are,

For the rest of your life, you, I'll guard

I promise I'm not trying to be trite,

But, I know we'll go really far

It may not be in fortune and fame,

But our love will be long, deep, bright.

Our love is like a bottomless jar.

We'll be together just the same,

Even if the whole world stops.

We'll walk 'till we have no more sight.

THE GAME OF LIFE

Why is it that America's pastime

Has become America's punchline?

It stands for what has made this country great.

Indeed, it's a game that holds immense weight.

Standing in the box, one thing in mind

With the support of a team behind.

In life you can fight 'til you breathe your last.

In baseball 'til the other team you've surpassed.

Life takes focus and determination.

To hit you need that and concentration.

To succeed in life you got to swing hard.

And to jack one you gotta swing without guard.

So next time they say baseball is not relevant

Speak up and show some wise dissent.

APPRECIATION FOR YOUR PERSPECTIVE

Thank you for not

Writing me off simply

Like all the rest.

Their ignorant, idle words

You just never bought.

They said that I was really

A flirt, lazy, a mess

A house of cards

That had no filter.

Because you gave me

A chance, you know clearly

Their words lacked truth,

They even lacked kilter.

Now you see me

Like few will ever see.

Now you will get

Something I gladly gave

You purely and free.

All I wanted was to be

Understood, met.

But few will others save.

To lower to a knee.

Reach out, love me

Where I was, and let

All preconceptions fade.

TIPPING

He didn't get my drink within a minute.

My water had too much ice in it.

His smile was mysteriously big.

15 Ketchups. Does he think I'm a pig?

He didn't light up my dining experience.

And he is lacking in appearance.

I'm sure he's made plenty today.

It's just one table anyway.

Here's examples of what some might say.

I'll leave a quarter without even blushing.

I don't even feel bad leaving nothing.

I don't mind leaving five percent.

Leaving fifteen would be too intense.

Most servers do their very best.

Most work without a second's rest.

They put up with absurdity and stupidity.

Must answer questions with no validity.

And through it all, they smile, rush around,

And treat you like you're the king of Burger Town.

UNFORTUNATE FRIEND SITUATION

Recently I decided to call a friend

And tell him of my awful week.

Tell him my struggle has no end.

That others treat me like a freak.

The harder I try to not be alone,

The more rejection I experience.

I know I'm grown and shouldn't groan.

And I don't want to put up a giant fence.

So I'll stay open and call that pal.

Tell him that I feel unseen and small.

In this I will move forward, I shall.

Then it hit me--I have no friend to call.

God is on my team

With him I will overcome

And I won't stay down

America's news

Who decides what they cover?

Hard to even care

Hello, St. Louis, MO

In the Bible Belt but why

Are natives so rude?

Pittsburgh

Place amidst forests

Nice buildings, parks, stadiums

I want to go back.

Boston

Rents like in New York

The city of patriots

And big tea parties

Toronto

Majestic 'scrapers

Like New York in Canada

Wealthy, diverse, bright

St. Louis Cardinal fanatics

Who are better fans

In all of sports than Cards fans?

They loudly show Card

Pacers Game

Your fans rival all

The Heat want to stay away

Huge home advanage

New York

I think you are great.

Charm, lights, huge parks, adventure

Best place on the globe

Baltimore

You gave us Babe Ruth

And the Star-Spangled Banner

Ravens, Orioles

Philadelphia

That letter to George

Cracked bell, fans that love to hate

An icon of us

Lonely but Hopeful

Too often I'm alone

No one to see or laugh with

I don't give up hope

Taking Down an Excuse Put up

I will make it up

No. The only thing you'll make

up is excuses.

INFORMATION AND FOOD

It's called the Information Age

Then why are so many clueless?

Inept often yet want a higher wage.

All this info yet the world's a mess.

Here are some theories as to why.

People go home, watch hours of TV

And eat a fair share of apple pie.

Pay raise equals spending spree.

Let's review the points I make.

Learning not valued, but food is.

Television 'til no longer awake.

Is this cycle really part of our biz?

Of course it is, and I even have a cure.

Let's yearn, not spurn knowledge.

Other nations are lapping us for sure.

Let's not party too hard through college.

Let's not eat until we want to puke

Let's not expect Big Brother to raise the pay.

Then we'll succeed and not look like a kook.

FOOTBALL

Is football just the game where grown men

Run around and try to hold a leather ball?

Or is it just the game where you try to get

The ball in that thing called the end zone?

On a smaller scale is it where you try to

Gain ten yards in three or four chances?

Or is it the ultimate game where you

Protect your teammates' backs in battle?

Indeed it is the latter, where you fight

For sixty minutes for success through pain.

And when you finally touch that victory

You can lie down with peace of mind.

The popularity of the sport will remain strong,

As teams continue converting third and long.

DALLAS COWBOYS

This verse is about football instead

Of about herding men on horses.

These Cowboys people love to hate

And love to jeer when they fail.

These Cowboys know this truth:

Win or lose, the nation will talk.

A team that peaked in the nineties,

Constantly attempts to peak again.

The quarterback with ten nicknames

Can win any week without praise.

Then get ripped apart by the masses

For a loss where he tried too hard

And came up just a hair short.

Some still believe that man, Romo,

Can win it all with the Cowboys.

Here's why they believe:

Romo can take an average team

And make them look All-World.

TULSA

It's the city many residents like to hate.

And so often times fail to appreciate.

It's the city where oil and gas booms

And half the year a twister eerily looms.

Cheap to live well and pay the bills.

The city with its fair share of thrills.

The huge fair makes heart rates increase.

World-class art at Philbrook and Gilcrease.

The city home of faith and Oral Roberts U.

You can go up Citiplex for a fantastic view.

The city that has a church on "every block."

This exaggeration people always like to mock.

In closing, it's a place you will likely crawl back to,

The song "Take Me Back to Tulsa" eternally true.

WHY WASTE LIFE

Why do so many people waste their lives?

For some it's fun and video games.

For others it's alcohol and drugs.

At the same time neglecting their wives.

Soon their loves are up in flames.

Inquiries are always met with shrugs.

Since they never stop to think deeply.

They easily lose focus and miss the mark

They forget we have exactly one life.

Their time always spent on thrills, cheaply.

Some see the fun really keeps their life dark.

So let my questions carve like a knife.

Since you have one life and only one,

Why do you live like you'll never die?

Do you think that your life is already won?

One day, I promise, we'll all say good-bye.

MONEY, MONEY, MONEY

If I got a dollar for every song out there

That glorified money I'd be uncleanly rich

Supposedly, if you have enough money

You automatically have happiness.

The wise ones reading this know

That this thinking is foolishly false.

Of course money oftentimes

Can make life easier, less stressful.

Too little money can make life

A little bit harder than you'd like.

Too much money and you might find

That you've changed to something

That you never wanted and don't like.

Those honest out there,

You, can tell me the answer

Doesn't money rank like fifth or so

In most important things in life?

God, family, friends, peace,

Contentment, purpose, joy.

Then money.

Okay, it's not even fifth.

SOME GUY I USED TO CALL A FRIEND

This is about a former friend, Stuart, who when he didn't like something
he'd hide.

When young, he'd hide from basketball.

I would search everywhere for him and call.

Tuesday, I came to visit while he hid up in the hall.

After he hid this last time I decided with a guy like that I can't and won't
abide.

IGNORANCE AND LAUGHTER

I think it's not wise to be bitter when people underestimate and harshly judge.

For ignorance can be found always, anywhere.

They told me in life you're pretty much a square.

And when I told a joke, they'd frown, giving a glare.

This criticism will make me crack up and I won't hold even a slight grudge.

KYLE OR SOMETHING

He and I were best friends for years.

But when he met his wife he went away.

His apathy towards me was very clear:

Our friendship rapidly began to decay.

Excuses like, "I don't like to talk on the phone."

Not sure what changed him so drastically.

I would ask to hang; he would internally groan.

To any inquiry I had, he met sarcastically.

But, friendship cannot be in words alone.

One day I told him he didn't need to pretend.

If he was my friend then start to act like one.

To that he left, and crossed me off as a friend.

To put it simply-as friends we were done.

REASESSING THINGS

underrated:

knowing the Creator,

dependable friends,

travelling the world,

being open to learning,

exploring nature.

OVERRATED:

GOING SHOPPING

POLITICAL CORRECTNESS

TAKING DRUGS

SCROLLING

HOLLYWOOD'S STANDARDS

BROKEN TO WHOLE

Innocence faded,

Now perception jaded.

Was bright-eyed,

Now black-eyed.

Time of fun and a game

Now horrific shame.

Life was understood and figured.

Now, life so huge, way bigger.

Trust between people broken

Pain and mourning unspoken.

Flagrant howling, even shaking.

Left alone, heart forever aching.

But, enter, One who has great loving care,

With a love so special, so unworldly rare.

The holy one who wants to wholly heal

And put back the light they tried to steal.

The love shared with masses--this love, real.

Life before complex,

Now no ill-effects.

Tears and weeping,

Now ecstasy sweeping.

HORROR MOVIES

Why do some find the need to view

Movies that send chills through their bones?

Every weekend millions march on cue

To see flicks full of victims' fruitless moans.

The "good ones" make hearts pound

The "bad ones" are predictable and unscary

"Good villains" can punish without a sound.

"Bad villians" do silly stuff, never necessary.

Some people's take on horror movies is this:

Life is pretty hard and frightful sans horror.

In fact, life sometimes is a downright abyss.

Remaining tearless often itself a hard chore.

FAMILY AND THE EMPIRE CITY

There is nothing quite like a son and father

Seeing captivating New York City together

Meeting up in midtown at scenic Bryant Park

Discussing going on a boat tour on the Shark

Learning of its important women and men

Riding a boat under the bridge to Brooklyn

Viewing the great architecture, a fair share

Eating local food at a café in Times Square

Going on a vessel by the symbolic Lady Liberty

Experiencing the city that most agree is pretty

Times like these you remember all your days

Even in dark times going through life's maze

SOCIAL MEDIA MISHAPS

Facebook

So many faces and friends, yet you still feel lonely

Snapchat

Many lively pictures and texts; your heart remains stony

Instagram

All this sharing you do, yet still nobody gets you

Twitter

Followers galore; still no desire to follow through

LinkedIn

Virtual connections you learn don't mean authentic

Pinterest

Seeing a perfect fake world pinned, now schizophrenic

Tinder

Find a date but all the while losing dignity and pride.

How can a world stressing social media remain so cruel?

The internet can't give you joy, friends or make you not a fool.

If you feel unfulfilled now, you'll remain so after you social mediate

Post, share, boast, view, pretend, befriend, pin, and date

A TRUE FRIEND I ALWAYS DREAMED OF, I THOUGHT

Finally one who won't stray.

This is a friend who will stay.

He will not leave and ignore

Like so many have done before

Texts sent will be returned.

My views won't be spurned.

Someone with who I can be me.

We can converse and be free.

Perceptions so many times untrue

One day, he's gone without a clue.

Having many pals is often overrated.

Realizing this, I'm no longer deflated.

US ON THE MOUNTAIN

Up here so many perfect things exist

Fun, laughs, freedom, nature, airy mist

Together we are on top of this world

Just hours ago our thoughts swirled

Much tries to hold us back in life

We choose not to fall into the strife

Hands held we climb the mountain

And this, my dear, you can be certain:

Even when we're not on the top of all

We will be steady avoiding a big fall

So let's sit and watch the sun go down

After, we'll go enjoy the glowing town

MAY AND YOU

It's hard to remember the pains of today

Gazing across the land this day in May

Sun rays, nature's flower arrangements,

A sudden rush comes of joyous content

Yet a single item is lacking I feel within

My love, confidant, one with a silly grin

I know that she would complete the scene

The one with who I haven't borders between

And as I begin to really wish for her presence

The one who has a love for me so immense

The horizon produces a beautiful being

I know there's nothing I'd prefer seeing

SAND

Hold, sift, caress

Or enjoy the view

A natural item that is

Like me and you

Sand amply can express

Characteristics of us

Pliability, grittiness,

Beauty, Softness

Let's leisurely walk

In the warm sand

With pleasant talk

Hand linked in hand

Examining what it is

That makes us grand

As our joy together rises

OUR LIKES AND I LIKE YOU

Can you really explain why it is we are so happy together, my little friend?

Maybe 'cuz we like the same things

Like silly jokes, dancing, rainy springs,

Deep canyons, hiking, and high swings.

Maybe one day things will progress to vows as we follow this upward trend.

SNOW MEMORIES

Snow down crawling

Now onslaught falling

So stunning, so serene,

So impeccably clean

Large feelings elicited,

Memories now revisited

Of that giant snow-storm

Meeting the girl so warm

Desire to know her deeply

Comprehend her completely

I'm so glad she accepted me

Did not turn away and flee

Now I get to hold her tight

Admiring winter's delight

A LITTLE PERSPECTIVE

Wait, just wait until life does change.

The more time that you hold on the

Higher chance of fortune exchange

Jobs do unfailingly fall through, uh

It's time to wake up for the grind

Eat a meager meal, look for work

Try not to get down from this bind

Try to see through the daily murk

Don't get stuck on the simple fact

That you don't have a bed or home

Think what you promised, the pact

That you wouldn't hopelessly roam

You would cling to the faith that your

Surroundings would turn around

At last your flailing would find shore

And guess what? You have been found

Now you're ready to take off and soar.

A REFERENCE FOR WHEN WE DRINK TEA

Here's a reference to look at when

You wonder what I love about you.

Your total being is a perfect ten.

You give in a way that so few do

And don't put much value on stuff.

You are a true womanly lady though

You're not a weakling—you're tough.

You're one who always looks to grow.

Your adventurous side excites me

As I look forward to our excursions.

On the bulk of life issues we agree.

So let us realize all our ambitions

As we sit by the fire drinking tea.

PHOENIX

The city named after that over-

Cited bird from Greek mythology

The heat will make you not sober

"It's just a *dry heat* is what we

Have," the residents say in gabber

Where having a pool, you'll see,

Is actually the norm here.

Vast metropolis, suburban city

Mesa, Scottsdale, Goodyear,

Gilbert, Glendale, and Tempe

Just to name a few. In fact, know:

If you meet a person from Arizona

Then he is likely from the metro

Here these find a mecca:

Cattle, Citrus, Cotton,

Copper, and Climate.

The Valley of the Sun--

For so many a warm fit.

DO, LOVE, AND LOOK

A wise man once said to be happy,

You need something to do,

Have someone to love,

And something to look forward to.

It's so simple, it's so true.

How many do not do much?

How many don't really love?

And don't look beyond today?

Choose today to

do, love, and look.

AN ODE TO A SPECIAL BIRTH

Christmas is not just about

The one day in December.

Some get enraged and shout.

"It's not the correct time of year

When Jesus was born!"

But let's not get snared

On this silly thorn.

God up above cared

So he gave us His Son.

Born from a woman,

But completely God.

He came from heaven;

Shepherds were awed.

They ran out of room

For the birth of him,

But Mary's groom

Didn't become grim.

He was born in a humble stable.

His life story impacts us all;

It is not a concocted fable.

Trust and see heaven's sprawl.

A DEEP CUT

What can hurt

More than being

Hurt by family?

Issues they know

Can allow them

To cut deep.

Today I got

Slit so deep--

I felt lifeless.

It felt surreal.

Will I choose

To forgive him?

THANKSGIVING AND DISTRACTIONS

Being thankful isn't just about one day;

Every morning we can wake and pray,

Even those with comparatively less

Have much to Him they can express.

Those without houses and money,

Still possess free-will and eternity.

So let's not from gratefulness stray

And get held up by work and play

And with how we appear and dress,

And with whom we can slickly impress.

For even when life isn't lively and sunny

You may find something at least funny.

INTRINSIC STUFF

Being heard

Being received

Being understood

It is so basic

And it so key

So intrinsic

Don't need lots

But at least 1

For you child are

Not an island

Neither is life

A popularity contest

Life is about finding the balance

It about not cutting ourselves off

But of finding one who can listen

A PEP TALK

The hardest things to do and not do in life

Often tend to be the most beneficial

Like being graceful and without strife

Being the true you and not the artificial

Choosing loyalty, always remaining man and wife

Not being covetous, but being simply grateful

All these choices often add up to a wonderful life.

IF YOU PLAY, THEY WANT YOU TO PAY

Two infamous renunciations,

That seemed impossible to be undone--

Were carried out by Peter and Judas.

Judas greedily betrayed God's Son

For thirty coins—such a small price--

Then could not find a way to go on.

Peter fearfully denied Jesus thrice,

But three days later found redemption.

In Acts, God used him as a potent device

After wrongdoing we select our direction

Will Judas or Peter act as our advice?

Behold, hope is found in the resurrection.

If You Play, They Want You to Pay

Today a man could not fathom

That at this certain establishment,

One must make a purchase

Before using the facilities.

He started out his diatribe

Whining like a child,

Which rapidly turned to

Demanding like an executive.

It swiftly developed into

Threatening like a bully.

The final act for the thespian:

Cussing like a mariner.

He disappeared as quickly as he came

Apologies from employees

To patrons lingered in the stagnant space.

MOMENTUM

It's as easy to get rolling forward

As it is to start spiraling backward.

Positive action leads to positive result

And

Poor choices lead to poor outcomes.

Likewise,

As it has been said before:

We never stay in one spot.

Today, which way will you roll?

Driving Force

What is driving our existence?

Why are we here?

Is it to survive due to being fittest?

If the chief goal is to survive,

Then death is a horrific defeat.

So, is empathy for man our true drive?

While empathy is noble, it does not

Lead to deliverance and fellowship divine.

Is our main purpose to love our Creator?

Yes. Our main purpose is to love Him--

With all our heart, soul, and mind.

AMERICA—YESTERDAY, TODAY, AND TOMORROW

Why does man struggle perpetually

With dark conduct and a bleak reality?

Inside, it's hard-wired to be wrong morally

Yet truth is snuffed with cocky certainty

The truth too inscribed on scrolls anciently:

Truth about God's exact personality

That of mercy and abundant redemption

This kindness brings us to repentance

And freedom from sin and iniquities.

America-Yesterday, Today, and Tomorrow

In 1886, the decree from our core

Like a beckoning shade tree.

Give me your tired, your poor,

Your huddled masses yearning to be free

And come they did with vigor

Now fear clothes the settled persons

A rigid clamor of desired rigor

Rules to protect his and her sons

With barns full and vats that gush

A nation with its beloved guns

Something ominous rises, a hush

The present and future face-to-face

Will we choose to give from our gifts?

Will the huddled masses be dealt grace?

Or will we cling to our own sacred space?

A NEW SEASON OF HUES

Leaves falling

Autumn awakening

Fall calling

Oranges, yellows, and reds

Soon

Nature's hibernation

And

Winter's white precipitation

ANIMALS THAT AMAZE

Beasts of the sea

Beasts of the sky

Beasts of the land

Beasts not so beastly

Creation breathed from on high

Sculpted by a majestic hand

Resemblance impossible to miss

The lioness' protection of her pride

A seal's celebrated playing in the sand

Two monkeys sharing an elated kiss

An old dog refusing to leave master's side

The blue jay singing a song so grand

Beasts going forth in perfect bliss

LOVE THAT CROSSES THE DIVIDE

I lie here in this empty space

Scantly able to look you in the face

Though when I do I find grace

A million things I regularly chase

But rarely you

The one who gets me through

This oftentimes disappointment of a life

The utter failure of the world rich in rife

But it was never your desire

Of us, only one thing you require

Our hearts-

It's where it all starts

And ends

For your love extends

Past our unrelenting blood loss

To the power of the cross

PROSPECTS AWAKENING

A new appearing chance

The opportunity to dance

What will the verdict be?

Will your life for once be free?

The choice is for you to make

To let yourself become awake

Will it be more of the same?

Or will you ready, set, aim?

NO LONGER WALKING WITH CHICKENS

You got away from the hindering group

You broke free of the sultry place

You flew out the filthy poultry coup

You splendidly left without a trace

Before, you ran around as if headless

No longer there--only by grace

Still have some but not nearly the stress

Totally free of the uncourageous crowd

What you do now is anyone's guess

Now free of the cumbersome cloud

I FEEL INSIDE SO HOLLOW

So much pain to have pride to swallow

Take some time to simply grieve

At it so long no longer naïve

My heart hangs out in craters, Apollo

But, enough with the self-pitying wallow

Self-doubt down the abyss I heave

Ready to gloriously achieve

Ready to give a command

Ready to nobly stand

Ready to walk in my purpose

Ready to shoot and not miss

SING!

Gonna sing until my cords are sore

Gonna dance until my muscles cramp

Gonna cry out from my inner core

Gonna light the midnight lamp

Gonna sing out in spirit and in truth

For the kingdom belongs

To those such as the youth

So, childlike I will sing songs

My desire is to love you

The way you love humanity

And Lord, know this is true

I no longer seek vanity

No longer gonna be what I do

PAPER, VAPOR, AND CAPERS

All hail Great Mr. Green

All bow for the mighty paper

The thing so pure and pristine

That inspires many a silly caper

Money: it hides and we seek

The legend of it like sweet vapor

In our minds, so pretty and sleek

Yet, by seeking, our lives taper

And prospects become bleak

CARING FOR THE DOWNTRODDEN

Gazing into the face of a down soul

Giving makes love generously broaden

And for hearts to be made whole

For eyes to move off yourself

Off your castle atop the knoll

Off your trophies on the shelf

Away from your safe fox hole

And stop loving so hard thyself

Look up, oh tunnel-visional eyes

And see the masses that gladly rise

THE LIFE BALLOT

Vote with your life

You may support life

On the ballot and online

But do you back her who

Births the child in despairing times?

Does your marriage model

Christ and the church?

Or when it comes to

Marriage your only care

Is who can't marry whom

As in a groom and a groom.

Do you love your guns,

Unconditionally?

Having a gun or a few

May not even save you.

People that love each other

Might be what allows safety.

Instead of worrying who lives

In the White House

Why not care more about living

A life of honor, giving,

Acceptance and peace and

Not one of hot air presumption

Judgement and lack of gumption.

Is your default argument

"They didn't try enough"

Or is it

"Freely you have been given

So freely give?"

Vote with your life.

BROKEN

Said I would

But didn't

Broke your trust

I leave now, I must

It's not meant to be

Now go be free

You will overcome

We both will

If I'm honest

From here it's the best

I foresee

Fly away my little bird

Too late, now that

I broke my word

A cord of two strands

So easily broken

God should have been

Our third cord

LIFE AT FULL-FORCE

You drilled a hole in my chest

And ruined my heart

I gave you my best

Your cruel doing just the start

Treated me like your pest

You sly, wicked, and smart

So long was oppressed

My heart your ugly canvas, art

You're gone, so now I rest

Sad to say this part

My victory the best

From a purposeful bullet

That sliced your evil crest

Your brain soaking wet

Victoriously, I find new zest

You perished, my life now reset

HIS ACTION AND OUR CHOICE

What Christ completed on the cross

Allows for cleansing of the hindering dross

His pain unlocked the locked door

Let there be a rebirth of our core

Behold One outside who waits

One who allows us into his gates

Will we hold onto our arrogance?

Or let Christ transform our essence?

Today what will we choose?

To pass the test or eternally lose

STEWARDS

When much is given much is demanded

For a wise man once commanded

That one must be a good overseer

Regardless of your ability tier

Something, anything must be done

Cannot despise your gift and run

Or hide it like the sinful servant

In a perfect world, our lives be fervent

We look to God and aim to please Him,

Whether we write, perform, teach, or swim

I NEED MORE

You're pretty

Eye-catching

But

You don't think

Worst

You don't care

to even think

You are boring

Nothing complex

I need Visual

And

Mental stimulation

It's not you

It's me

I think

The end

WATCH OUT FOR CERTAIN GROUPS

If you like to talk and *have* fun

And you're in a big group *look* out

Happens so often, repeatedly *done*

No point to frown, look-down and *pout*

If you tell a joke, some will blankly stare

Just like If you do something edgy or fun

So, don't give them time, you're rare

People often are fun-Nazis with a gun

Life can sometimes mirror Facebook

People search to be upset with pouty looks

When you find one of these groups run

These folks will rob you ragged like crooks

Their joy comes from having no joy or fun

EVERY HUMAN CAN APPRECIATE

Thankfulness of which to sing

Hundreds of things we could all count

Even the person in the Far East

With the absolute least

Would have so much

For which to give thanks

Next time you want to complain

Do not.

Say thank-you instead.

FAITHFULNESS

God knows all about

Your issues and pain

Of your suffering and

Internal stains

He desires to reach down

And gently meet you.

Not always when we want

But always on cue.

When some were starving

He sent manna and quail.

He did not allow his people

To be sickly and pale.

When his people were trapped

With nowhere to go

He parted the waters, so his

Protective hand they could know

When there seemed no way

For His people to win

He knocked down the walls

And ushered victory in.

When others pushed away the

Lepers and other untouchables

Jesus met them, healed them,

And revealed himself capable.

Next time you're losing hope,

Not knowing what to do,

Raise your eyes up and

Trust God will deliver you too.

FROM A HARD PAST TO A BEAUTIFUL FUTURE

All the pain from the difficult past

He brought you ahead, it all passed

As much as you could possibly care

He cares more, wants to spare

Spare you from the scars.

Past issues can be shining stars.

Your bleak past leave behind

And trust the Father so kind.

THAT WAS CLOSE (OR WAS IT)

When it seems you're going no where

And the answers you don't know where

Then don't give away your dignity, don't cede

The potential for growth is there, now it's a seed

To fit in, they tell him what is not allowed

His frustrations grow til he erupts aloud.

They call him dull, out of the loop, plain

So, he wants to fly from the group on a plane

Always say in the head he's just not right

So, he stays up late to ponder and write

Later, glad he didn't sell his soul to the joyless band

Had he, his joy would have essentially been banned

A FINAL NOTICE OF US

You stabbed me twice and turned the knife

Showed total disregard for my very life

Before that I didn't even try to hurt you

I took care of you the best that I knew

You misconstrued my actions and motive

You thought I selfishly placed myself above

However, that was not remotely the case

I wondered why you never look me in the face

The broken pieces of us are here for all to see

Pardon me as I try to reassemble the pieces of me

NO ONE LIKE YOU

When all left, you said you would stay

When I needed you, you came through

You still loved me, when I forgot to pray

You don't condescend, that's why I love you

Decapitated, you have been my crutch

I've learned from all the trials and each test

But our togetherness together is as such:

Your love radiates from my very chest

And makes me holy and clean to the touch.

HIGH PRAISE

When I was searching for hope

Was looking for belonging and love

My fingers barely grasping the rope

Even sought help from above

God sent me, He sent me you

You helped me heal and set me free

Life now is a total different view

I'm able to be my best me

Able to experience life anew

You unlocked me, you beautiful key

OLD HABITS DIE HARD (OR NOT AT ALL)

People don't change

70's, 80's, 90's, and 2000's

So, don't find it strange

If you trade their phones

And Giant televisions for

Rotary phones and analog tubes

Always surpassing the Jones'

Lack of follow through

And broken promises too

Excuses aplenty flow

Around now and

Just as much decades ago

Trust built on sink sand

YOU ARE GREAT

It's not you,

It is them.

All of them.

Pretty much on cue.

Until promises are valued

And selfishness disregarded

Perpetual sameness will remain

And be an emotional drain

A TALE AS OLD AS TIME

A smooth seductress

Stole his naïve heart

That cunning abductress

It was his gift at the start

When she wore that red dress

His destiny shrunk like with a dart

His life quickly turned a mess

Was not clever or close to smart

Liberation when he did confess

To the one hurt, his sweetheart

A PEP TALK FROM A CHURCH ON A HILL

What does your heart beat for?

What makes it beat faster?

What makes your heart soar,

Makes you euphoric to the core?

Whatever it is, do that more.

Whether it's a verb or a noun,

Don't let life get you down.

Pursue it with all you can

And don't be a life also-ran

Be a champion and fearless leader

Not an unhappy bottom-feeder

Don't let circumstances determine it

Go out and joyfully show grit

Never lose hope, never quit

PEOPLE OF OLD SHOWING US THE WAY

Let Christians today be more like Daniel of old,

Who stood in faith regardless what was told,

Who prayed on behalf of a lost people group,

Who didn't hear a bad report and let his heart droop

Like Jesus who cried out as he suffered, "Lord forgive them"

And Like the woman who just strove to touch Jesus' hem

And like Caleb who said "Let's go up for we are well able"

Let's teach those who think the gospel a fable.

Let's seek God and not just what is in His hand,

Who are strong and courageous and take a mighty stand.

MORE, MORE, MORE

Consumption today consumes us

Chews us up and spits us out

More blessed to give than receive

But why are we so easy to deceive

We collect stuff so devout

How did it come to this?

The American dream so full of bliss

I say this with absolutely no doubt

If there is no change, we won't survive

We sure as anything won't continue to thrive

Just ask the Babylonians, Persians, or Romans

You can change when you see the signs

Or do nothing about these perilous omens

If nothing done, the collapse will be a spectacle

And the world will observe, "What a debacle."

MY CHILDREN, KNOW YOUR GRIT

My daring son, go for it

My daughter, know your grit

I raised you to be like me

To not hold back, but be free

It is not in your nature to fear

So this I must tell, my dear

Be very strong and very proud

Hold your head high, lead the crowd

When you don't know how to act

Do your best and that is a fact

My children, come to me and be near

Don't listen when others mock and jeer

My dear children, go for it

My children, know your grit

FREEDOM WILL COME

When what you say is twisted

And your face gets hit, gets fisted

Your intentions become misaligned

And you find it hard to keep your mind

Just hold onto your patience and wits

Showing poise will give the adversary fits

You will then find happiness unassisted

And your freedom will not be confined

But instead fulfilled, full of hope and ritz

Never giving up, never calling it quits

INTANGIBLES OVER TANGIBLES

In the end, there is no trophy for stuff

No matter how much for it you competed

To rack up things even when the going got tough

At the pearly gates, you won't be better greeted

At some point, you have to say "enough"

If you strive for stuff your intangibles will be depleted

So, go for depth and avoid the hollow fluff

Find what is unnecessary and what actually needed.

PEOPLE: A SNAPSHOT

People suck

Are mean

Selfish and dumb

However,

God

Made them

Our job

Is to

Love them

And not

Judge them

A LITTLE NOTE

Hello,

We used to be friends

I thought this note I would send

So you could at least think of me

One more time

I'm sorry it didn't work out

That I talked when you wanted a mime

That I graduated being a weakling, grew stout

I thought I'd check in to show you my success

This all may make you sniffle and pout

When I was with you I was a mess

Seeing me will make you envious no doubt

I come here for truth, not to impress

Pardon me as I flow out of my freedom spout

Signed,

A baseball player on a field of bread

DARK VIOLENCE TO FREEDOM

Drilled a hole in my chest

And ruined my heart

Made it gush like dark oil

Made blood hot like a broil

Filled completely with hollowness

Made you see them for what they are

All their inglorious shallowness

The depths of depravedness

Hard to fathom

Their Hades stratum

Come up now I will

Having remnants of life still

YOU SEE PAST MY FAULTS

You set me free

And you call me

Man of valor

Man of vigor

Man of honor

Yet I feel like a goner

Lord, do you know

The places I go

And what I've done

I expect you to shun

Yet, you show me grace

Seeking me like in a chase

You have set me apart

So today is a new start

GRACE TO THWART PREJUDICE

Whether you do agree or disagree

All our experiences are not bias-free

We can really try and do our very best

Trying hard to succeed at the racial test

We can do our best to racism thwart

But at the end of the day we fall short

It really and honestly is as simple as this

'Til we find His love we will miserably miss

Until we turn the love to grace for another

We will struggle with our very brother

You can spend weeks in sensitivity training

But your accepting will still just be feigning

Let God's dear love wash your hostile heart

And begin to love all and today you can start

HEED WHEN HE CALLS

When the Word of the Lord comes, be advised

Lest, God shows up and his actions are unrealized

When the Word came to Elijah he was told to hide

In Ezekiel 28, the Word came to rebuke pride

The Word told Abraham about his anticipated heir

When it came in Ezekiel 12, it was to prepare

When it came to Jonah, it was for him to preach

To Isaiah, the Word came to show His ways and teach

When the Word of the Lord comes now will you heed it?

Or will you harden you heart like the lazy steward and sit?

LOVE HARDER THAN THE WORLD

Blssed are you my obedient servant

You took in and cared for the broken woman

You valued the man the world called wild

You brought to your home the fatherless child

And took him in as your precious very own

Looked after him till he was all grown

Draw near and accept your golden crown

For eternity, you will rule over a town

Because you cared for what I care for,

Brought heaven down as when the curtain tore

I will honor, extol, and glorify you

For you have loved like few of my people do

A PRODIGAL AND A KING

When the world saw me in the sewer

You failed to see me only as the wrong-doer

When even I saw myself going nowhere

You saw me through, showed me your care

When the world cursed my name

You brought me past my enormous shame

I look to you my blessed, radiant King

For you adorned me with a robe and ring

Saying, "My son was lost, but now he is found."

Loftily I soar, no more I cower on the ground.

THE FLEA AND THE FLY (CIRCA 2006)

Once there was a flea who sat on a fly

The fly said, "Flee and say good-bye."

But the flea said, "No, dawg, I wanna stay."

So the fly found a frog to get it away;

And when the frog stretched out his tongue,

The flea was taken down away—

The fly was forced to go along.

THE PENETRATING EYE (CIRCA 2006)

Look, the eye of the Lion,

And it's staring you down.

The all-knowing, penetrating eye,

That shrewd look, making you fearful.

Like the moon in the sky,

Bright-shining, sometimes fateful.

THE MASK WE WEAR (CIRCA 2006)

O, what a mask we wear;

With it we hide all that is true

And noble and important to us.

With it we try to copy

Those we think "cool" or good.

So let us take it off,

to reveal our scars, color, and tears.

Take it off.

Look, you conquered your fears.

GREEN GRASS GROWS (CIRCA 2006)

Grass, grass, oh so green;

Money, too, of that color.

Both share the bond of value.

Grass, a vital part of nature—

We must realize true wealth.

THE SKY AND LIFE

The vast blueness over our heads--the sky

Sometimes with clouds, at other times not.

It sends surprises that deeply touch us,

Just ask the weatherman.

Life is like the sky—

Endless possibilities and color.

REST AND ART TO BEAT THE STRUGGLE

Plodding, flailing, barely treading

Right when you think it's subsided,

Life comes back full-fledged, revenging.

A solution to this fright here is listed:

Find a method where you find rest.

For some it's sport, for others, art.

Find that which keeps you your best.

For with no outlet life may fall apart.

So next time you come home stressed,

Release, then wake up to a fresh start.

REASONS TO BE THANKFUL

Thankfulness of which to sing

Hundreds of things

We could all count

Even the person in the furthest East

With the absolute very least

Would be able to count so much

For which to give forth thanks

Next you want to complain

Instead give thanks for things like rain

A HAIKU ABOUT MAN'S PLIGHT

Mankind in shambles

The Savior child was given

Be whole, forgiven

A JOYOUS OCCASION

Heaven's best sent as a gift and prize

To fill us with light and to lift our cloudy eyes

God's one and only son to save us all

To rectify the first Adam's fateful fall

In a humble place, Heaven's Son was born

So that God's presence can us adorn

He was placed in an animal's manger

To connect us to God, no more a stranger

No longer must suffer indefinitely

Can be loved by our Father affectionately

So let us all come together and remember

Why we joyously celebrate in December

CHRISTMAS REASONING

Why even celebrate Christmas?

For so often the point we miss.

It represents God's present

In the form of His Son's descent

Let's move our focus off holiday stuff

And learn to say enough is enough.

Say only Jesus deserves my heart

And go to the beginning, the start

Joyfully singing out to Him Hosanna,

The One who supplies heavenly manna.

WHAT JESUS MEANS FOR THE WORLD

Behold the Savior is born in a stable

In 33 years, salvation will be available

Born to earthly parents, a heavenly Father above

Sent down like a spotless, beautiful dove

His life is the world's special example

Like grapes to wine the soldiers did trample

His consecrated life a sacrifice poured out

Offering eternal life when believing without doubt

He opened the door to relationship with the Creator

The One victorious and whose love is greater

Step forward and accept the Savior Child

And come before the throne reconciled

GOD'S CARE, THEN AND NOW

God knows about your issues and pains

Of your suffering and internal stains

He desires to reach down and melt you

Not always when we want, but on cue

When some starved, he sent manna and quail

He did not allow his people to be sickly and pale.

When his people were trapped with nowhere to go,

He split the sea, so his defending hand they could know.

When there seemed no way for his people to win,

He knocked down the walls and ushered victory in.

Next time you're losing hope not knowing what to do,

Raise your eyes up and trust God will deliver you too.

When others pushed away the lepers and untouchables,

Jesus met them, healed them, and revealed himself capable.

When you add up all the pain from the difficult past,

He parted the issues and brought you ahead, you passed.

As much as you could possibly or even want to care,

He cares even more for his child, wants to spare.

Spare you from the visible and painful scars,

That past issues can turn into shining stars.

Your bleak past, my child, leave behind

And trust the loving, caring Father so kind

GOD, PURE AND GIVING

Praise and worship the Lord,

Stop, stand, and adore.

Not seeking just his miracles,

Seeking the one Holy in essence and core,

The One gloriously unpredictable.

Lay down your worries from the start

And behold Him wash you clean,

Making your spirit and soul pristine.

A LIFE THAT FALLS SHORT

You watch TV to never be unprepared

When a pop culture reference is dropped.

You lift weights religiously regularly

To look nice, have the right image

You eat the right stuff they tell you to,

So your body always looks good as new

You treat your neighbor kindly.

Surface-wise you look happy, carefree

At night, you lie awake worried

Knowing there is a God you direly need

But you never make the connection

Never get yourself in the right direction.

You look great but miss God's protection

And never lay down your life to His redemption.

Without Jesus' forgiveness, you end up lost

Forever thrown around by life, always tossed

ABOVE THE HATERS

Swimming in success, Mark Spitz

Ignoring haters in the pits, give 'em fits

Going so dang fast, Mike Andretti

Dancing so hard, getting sweaty

People asking if all this will last

Putting the naysayers on blast

Made a name for myself

Picked myself off the shelf

Rising above the world, Neil Armstrong

Being this way can't be wrong

Destined for greatness, Apollo Eleven

Known my call since I was seven

Never losing my way, Hans and Gretel

Got standards, no more I will settle

Won't stop, keep my foot on the pedal

A STREAM, A SHELL, AND A KING

The best is yet to come

You will inherit it all, not just some

The king of glory has picked you

Has lifted you on high, behold the view

Ask, my child, and you shall receive

Just have a little faith and believe

For I am preparing where you will go

It will be beautiful how you will flow

Like a stream across a barren land

Like a spectacular shell in the sand

So, close your eyes and put faith in me

As today I emancipate you, forever free

THEY SHARE MISERY WITH OTHERS BUT NOT ME

Their misery now in common

Before it was their criticism

Their misery tried to birth misery in me

Their birthing system I did not examine

But I took control of my future and joy

Told them I wasn't their silly toy

I know it's cliché but now I am free

Like two peas in a snug little pod

Can keep each's cold heart warm

Their misery gets company

FIND YOUR PURPOSE

What fulfills you completely,

Makes your heart and mind free,

Makes your heart skip a beat?

Let opportunity and preparation meet.

Go do what your gifts dictate,

Don't just leave your life to fate.

Don't bury your gift in the ground.

Don't pound a square into what's round

Be dedicated, be fierce, and fervent

Well done, my good and faithful servant

HEART MATTERS

Does your heart follow your Master

Or is it stiff and cold like plaster?

Has our heart grown deathly lifeless?

Have you lost your fire, no longer fearless?

Do you daily disappoint your Father

When He tries to speak, you say, "Don't bother."

Today a voice in the street make a proposal

Will you be willing and at His disposal?

COMEDY COMPARED TO OTHER ARTS

Why do some choose to do stand-up comedy?

Maybe because hearing laughter is so pretty

Could be cuz of the crowd's happy vibe

The payoff for comedy is immediate

Find out fast if the jokes register and fit

In music, you succeed if you're highly sought

In acting, you find out when the film flops or not

In painting, it's if someone buys the piece

In most creative fields, feedback takes time

In comedy, you succeed 'til the laughs decrease

So get up there and bring people laughter

Until the applause echos from the rafters

ON THE WAY TO A MAGNIFICENT CITY

Driving to a favorite metropolis

Seeing the well-crafted skyline

Some so iconic impossible to miss

You feel connected like twine

Ideas of adventure cascading

Arrays of excitement come to mind

Ready to navigate, head-high parading

A MAN IN RED VS CHRIST

Santa is overrated

Santa Clause gives us presents

Christ, eternal life

LET'S GET IT RIGHT IN AMERICA

A nation founded on biblical principles and liberty

Yet, for a hundred years we reasoned having slavery

Another hundred years we oppressed those freed

The majority must have not viewed equality as a need

Even today we reason their struggle is a result of pride

The "ghettos" just remnant lines of where one could reside

And home loans were not given as they were to me and you

A white guy with weed gets charitable treatment and is let go

A Black guy with the same gets five years, don't you know?

A white man at the hospital gets superior care

A Black man gets care you could barely call fair

A white person gets called in for the interview

A Black person's chance of that is minuscule

A Black person that is on welfare is labeled typical

A white person on it is down on their luck and abnormal

So can we stop the narrative that racism in America is dead?

And, actually start addressing the truth we aren't usually fed?

Admitting the injustice is actually just the start

For lasting change has to come from the heart

A GLIMPSE FROM A TERRIBLE CAMP

Side crushed with a hammer

So weak can hardly stammer

Hunger pangs echo from head to toe

Despair and agony is all I know

Since I got to the concentration camp

Sleeping with two hundred, so cramped

Not sure my age, somewhere around 10

No idea if I will even leave or when

Dawn to dusk I work outside

Many days I wish I had already died

Alas, this story is from my early days

A picture of man's potential scary haze

We have come far in a lot of ways

Though evil forever with man stays

I will remember the camp's hateful craze

Yet, thankful I look up and give praise

PEOPLE THAT ARE VICIOUS

People don't like what is different

Different background, talk, dress, origin

These people can get quite unpleasant

You see them in action with an evil grin

Day in and day out they will bludgeon

Not caring about you or your anguish

Your distress and tears don't budge them

Peace and acceptance is your only wish

WHAT SOME SAY ABOUT HIM

He must not be too smart

Must not be ambitious

Must not have much in his heart

You're pretentious and capricious

Maybe I enjoy what I do

It pays the bills and gives freedom

How 'bout you judge yourself, too?

Does your life equal an ideal sum?

Are you following your dreams?

Clarity may to you one day come

I'm happy; judgmental you, isn't, it seems

THE GAME ON THE GRIDIRON

Months of anticipation for this

The juggernaut that football is

Every fan thinks this is the year

Telling any and all who will hear

Shout it out, it's finally football time

The fans chant in perfect unified chime

The crowds get riled with thundering noise

While wearing colors that further their voice

Uh oh, they scored on the opening kickoff

Too early to panic and slightly early to scoff

Now 21-0, other team, have yet to cheer

I'm ready for a nap; this will be a long year

HOW TO ACT AT COMEDY OPEN MIC IN THE US

Bring notes to show

Ignore other comics who are on stage

Listen halfway to a few jokes

Take smoke break

Do not laugh. Don't even think about it

Get on stage. Check notes a lot. Get a few half-laughs

Get off stage. Get fist-bump from friends. And?

Go out for smoke break. Then leave

Find comfort of own home that you share with five others

WILD TIMES, THE ILLEST

My brain so calm it could explode

At such peace, I sit in a busy road

Head in a hole, like it's my calling

An elderly honks, my serenity still not falling

Birds roar their merry approval

Oh boy, this is living

Picked up, a swift removal

A man in blue, generally quite giving

SOCIAL JUSTICE WORDIOR

Gotta change this country

Even the whole backwards world, set it free

These words not anti or pro PC

Just anti words alone

Anti typing gleefully into a phone

Anti your grumble and moan

Do something, anything

A nice thing or a hard thing

Not a word thing, but a verb thing

A (MODERN) FAIRY TALE

True love found from my heroic finger

I'm a prince and last night found Ms. Charming

We will have a child for each finger

If only we liked kids—this is alarming

My finger swipe led to a romantic test-drive

When Ms. Charming's feminine muscle car accelerated

I know she was this month's queen of the other five

Before my finger could swipe, dating I hated

Now I don't gotta send junk mail

And creep around, getting faded

This is a modern fairy love

THE LION, THE BEAR, THE GIANT

I find myself running towards a huge person

Deja vu

to a time I ran towards the lion

Who

Wanted to have a little lunch of lambs

And

the bear who wanted to snack on sheep

I overcame both, all glory to God

Now

I am prepared to face this giant

Who

Is named Goliath.

FRIENDS AND FAMILY

Take away friends and family,

And what do I have?

God, a little money and things.

But God is enough;

He loves all, and some love Him.

I love Him.

He is enough.

THE WORLD

I want to see the world

I want to love the world

The way God sees and loves

God, guide me where to go

Send me out like a flock of doves

So pure and untouched

The thrill of flying, travelling

I want to be like a dove

I want to be like God

Seeing and loving

DAYS AND THE LORD

Today was made by God

Just like Yesterday and

Tomorrow

Each day thoroughly a gift

I learn from the past,

Enjoy the present

And not worry about

The future

I give all three to God

To do as He wills

HOLDEN AND JANE

I stand before you today

With some simple things to say

I passionately adore you

I desire and need you too

You make me flutter

And sometimes I even stutter

Like a bird and a babbling brook

I'm now your open book

Your "The Catcher in the Rye"

I'm Holden, about to fly

Just waiting for your beautiful signal

You my angel, my mountain, my lovely symbol

My Jane, the one so good and pure

The medicine to my ailments, my lifelong cure

So, as I wait for your nourishing ointment

I'm full of hope as for a birthday present

Place it in my throat through my parched lips

As we sail together on side-by-side ships

Together, we will save those going off the embankment

Feeding the hungry, offering gentle encouragement

Clothing the naked, embracing the dying and hopeless

The lost ones, overlooked of perpetual crying

Those who for so long have felt voteless

The lost ones, overlooked and perpetual crying

We will give them wings until they are flying

INTO THE OCEAN AND THE WORLD

Take me to the ocean so vast

I want to step in and go crashing

New horizons, pain and fear past

My old me sprawling in fear, thrashing

The bright color of faith and hope burning

The sight of you—can't miss—the tallest mast

Strength of a warrior's spirit churning

The past me breathing his last

It's just me and you here in this moment

All worries, second-guessing, and the past I toss down

Into the uproarious and raging torrent

Out of all that, you present me a crown

Saying, to the dark and teary world, "You, I have sent"

And I respond, "Thank you for this white gown

For all your life and blood you spent

I am unworthy but so grateful

And you, so perfect and beautiful

A NEW CHAPTER

You, who I adore, have shown me

Such a kindness I could never imagine

A feeling of belonging and being free

It starts out slow, now a full-faced grin

Your affection for me is so lovely

Together, anytime and any place we can win

Our joy gushing together so bubbly

Hand-in-hanf we avoid tangling sin

My exclamations I promise not hyperbole

So now may our new merry chapter begin

WHAT YOU MEAN TO ME

When God made you, it was a special gift

When you said "Yes" to me, it was so special too

You are the helium that makes my heart lift

The one I love through and through

You have that special air about you

So rare, so precious, so beautiful

You are never late, but always on cue

Like the notes in a world-class musical

Inspiring, ravishing, sweet beyond belief

You stole my heart, you adorable thief

Now I'm brighter than ever, the greenest leaf

AGE OF EMPIRES

We see something that makes no sense

We get scared and want to tear it down

When I played as the Persians,

I wanted to tear down the Greeks

Cause that's what I read in my history books

And, when I went to learn about the new culture,

I was investigating to naturally one day come back

I looked suspicious to their watch towers,

Who sent single arrows, hordes of arrows or

No, please no, not the cannons.

My men are friendly I promise

Soon I sent in my troops that,

"If by the hand of God" was enough

I could finally, finally talk some reason and

Some common sense to them

And it didn't always work

Lord, where did you fail me?

Why is it so hard to live at peace with my fellow man?

His pretty gold so shiny and

Would have looked great being mined by

My blue men and my red men who

Simply loved their country,

But also, never stopped to ask,

"Why did I just turn my weapon into a pick-ax?

And the arms that held my dying and

Dead comrades are now the arms I cross when

I don't think my master/king/ruler and

Leader of hopefully the whole world one day,

Lord willing, since he really—

Connected to me, my family and my background

I stopped playing Age of Empires figuring it was time

To move on and be a real grown-up

So here I am today trying to process a game that

Is more real than I ever imagined.

THE ROAD

It gives me grief to say today

That you, Road, have too long

Been my grandest and truest friend.

I wish it were not as such.

For half (or so) of the good of life

Comes from finding they that care.

Most can talk of grand things:

By their valiant words of air

You'd think their very life they'd share.

Yet my heart of sadness sings.

It sings of longing for the highways,,

That winding, never ending stretch

Promising much like all the people.

But never knocks you to the byways.

But, here I am again in this familiar place.

Tears no more in this new found space.

For what I have found is not fickle and sly in speech.

I found You.

JOKES FROM ZANE HOLDEN TREFIELD (MANY OF THESE HAVE BEEN TOLD LIVE ON THE STAGE)

MISCELLANEOUS PERSONAL JOKES

I'm getting tired of my washing machine because I'll be chilling in my kitchen next to the utility room telling killer jokes and my washing machine never laughs. But then it says something hilarious like "rawww" like an adorable monster and then I'm dying laughing. But I'm like "Show ME some love, Maytag!"

It's tough when something you've thought your whole life comes toppling down. I've always seen myself as a strong Christian. But recently I looked at myself shirtless in the mirror. I was like, "I don't look Christian; I look like the founder of Buddhism. Though, my jelly rolls are not very Zen.

I've been doing comedy over 10 years, and for most of that time there was no success or anything to show for it. Lately, things have turned around. I ca n now afford 2-ply toilet paper. My boots is so clean. And, with all that thickness, I don't even have to wash my hands. I smell my fingers and I'm like, "That is the smell of success in comedy."

I'm a big Texas Rangers fan which is crazy because I don't usually like law enforcement.

I like to read my tortoise the story of "The Tortoise and the Hare," but he doesn't like it because he doesn't have hair." He's bald. He is a big fan of Malcolm Gladwell which for a turtle makes him an outlier.

I have a turtle. His name is Gus. He's a very fun guy. No he's a very Fun Gus. He's practically a mushroom.

MENTAL HEALTH JOKES

I have been to four mental hospitals in three states, not to brag. I think I want to go to one in all 50 states. I told that recently to my friend Matt and he was like, "Dude, that's craaaaaaaaazy!" I was like, "Bingo." I think I'd actually like to just go to Laureaute Hospital in Tulsa 50 times and become the Michael Jordan of Laureaute. "He's a 6-time arts and crafts champion, he puts up stats and makes his teammates better, and is a real treat in group therapy." When you're in a mental hospital, all you think about is getting out as fast as you can. And when, you're onstage, all you think about is how fun it was to have all that free-time. They've diagnosed me as bi-polar, but I think I just have an addiction to mental hospitals. I've been to mental hospitals in conservative and liberal states. In liberal states in the mental hospital, people are running around half-naked, doing yoga, and talking about their feelings. In conservative states in the mental hospital, they're just like "Take your meds and pray. But, really the first one isn't a big deal."

I don't think I'm crazy. At least that's what I'm told by the voices in my head.

The first time I got put in a mental hospital, we had snacks and then went outside and I got to play basketball. I thought it was gonna be "all fun and games." Boy, was I wrong.

BUS JOKES

Now, I drive a city-bus for Tulsa Transit, because they didn't give me a psych-eval. Now, on the bus, it's like the inmates are really running the asylum. "Sir, I think what you need is some Lexapro, but I'm no doctor, just the friendly, neighborhood bus-driver!

If you haven't ridden a city-bus, it's often a melting pot of mental illness. The bus has a lot of perverts, delinquents, and criminals…but enough about the drivers. Some of us are only two of those things and we get raises and good schedules. "Officer, I do know why you pulled me over—because there's 10 people with outstanding warrants in the back, and 1 in the driver seat." Most busses hold 40 people, but I was once full with 20 people, because everyone was saving a seat for their imaginary friend. It was half the fares, but twice the fun.

Recently , we got some driver barrier shields on the bus. I've noticed I'm whistling a lot more now. Cuz, I know "Why the Caged Bird Sings." He sings because he can't get assaulted anymore by "Big Mike."

On the bus, drivers can't listen to the radio, but sometimes in a rough neighborhood, we do get to hear the rhythm of gunshots. "It's a hard-knock life for us (bang, bang, bang); it's a hard knock life for us." (bang, bang, bang)

TRUE ONES THAT MAYBE GOT MADE UP

⌘

I'm friends with a guy named Roy. Full name is Roy G. Biv. Yep, he's on the spectrum. Of light. To be honest, he sort of is the spectrum.

If you guys don't want to follow me, I get it. Cuz, the last guy who did, got charged with stalking. Instagram, sir. Not, my house.

They had this 10 year old kid throw out the first pitch in St. Louis. Everyone cheered hard and I said, "Yeah, but can he tell a joke?"

Olive Garden's slogan is "When you're here you're family." My family's slogan is "When you're here, you're family. And, when you're not here, we gossip about you."

I've always wanted to have kids and I thought I had to get a wife to do that. Then I learned about IVF and being a single dad through a surrogate mother. So, no need to bother getting married. I know what you're thinking, and me too. "Why buy the chicken if you can get the eggs for a fee?"

As a kid, I lived in a yellow house on 2nd Street. Which gave me quite an inferiority complex. It got much better when I moved to 1st Street.

SOCIAL COMMENTARY AND OBSERVATIONAL HUMOR

In Oklahoma, they don't know what "toxic masculinity" is. They just call it "being a real man." Yep, and "boys will be boys" as long as free passes are handed out en masses.

You guys ever go to a kids' birthday party that has one of those bouncy houses? I've noticed the kids jumping inside give 0 cares about the kids trying to get in. The kid taking his shoes on is getting trampled. The kid trying to get through those flaps is getting knocked into. And the kids doing it are full of glee. "The cover charge is 5 stomps to the head or groin." Talk about some savage security. These are the world's smallest bouncers! (Pun intended to the nth degree)

Tulsa just got its first Black Mayor after 126 years. On a sad note, Tulsans have said that they will never pay out reparations for the Tulsa Race Massacre of 1921. I had a dream last night that reparations finally happened. They just burned down Gathering Place. White people were so ticked.

STAIRS ARE PROGRESSIVE.

A dog is a man's best friend. I think a cat could be a cows best friend because they both speak a similar language. One goes "moo" and the other goes "meow." And cats love milk.

Opioid crisis? More like Okieoid crisis! The Sooner we fix it, the better!

People who cracked "All Lives Matter" thought they were being so clever with their little joke. Not me. More like, "All Jokes Can't Be Winners."

"Sprinkles are for winners" is how the saying goes. The South needs to learn that "Heroes get statues; Confederate punks get nothing."

BIBLE AND RELIGION JOKES

Jesus was very popular when he was alive. People loved that he was so down-to-earth.

I was reading the Beatitudes. Jesus was saying stuff like, "Blessed are the poor in spirit, for they shall see God" and "Blessed are the meek for they shall inherit the earth" and "Blessed are the poor in music taste, for they shall be called hipsters."

The Bible says a day is like a thousand years and a thousand years is like a day. That makes Jesus two days old. I want to give the little guy a rattle, so he can make a joyful noise. "Goo goo, God, God."

I think God was trolling modern Christians when he made Jesus' first miracle turning water into wine and last teaching at the Last Supper was giving wine for communion. God is like, "How's that 'drinking is always a sin' working out for you? God has a sense of humor. I'd go to his show.

I wonder if God believes in Creationism? Like how sad would it be to be powerful enough to create the universe, yet not have enough faith to believe you actually did it? Jesus is like, "Dad, did you create the universe?" God is like, "Let me take the elevator down to consult my friend Charles Darwin. He's complaining of the heat but hopes it evolves to a better situation. I told him last time, 'not in a million years.'"

God in the Old Testament was pretty wild. God in the New Testament is chill and nice. You know what they say about guys getting a new perspective on life when they become a dad.

RANDOM JOKES

A person who can identify aromas in an aggressive fashion is called a sensei.

Guys, if you ask out a woman and she says she can't because she has to wash her hair, she thinks she's being pretty suave. Like compared to the other girls, she's head and shoulders above. She'll never drop her Pantene routine for you.

I had an epiphany today. Which was learning what the word "epiphany" means. Turns out, the other epiphany I had was that I'm not as smart as I thought I was.

Donald Trump as president is called "Commander in Chief." Commander in Chief? More like Commander Insurrectionist.

My cousin Will is addicted to protein shakes because "Where there's a Will, there's a whey."

I hung a picture today that says "Neigh." Boy, is it hung like a horse.

This guy was yelling "camouflage" or something. I couldn't really hear him.

Zane giving a special person a present from his heart.

The author as a child, doing what he loved, creating art.

The author with good friend, David, at a Red Sox game in Boston, MA.

The author on one of the best days of his life where he attended the Just For Laughs Comedy Festivals in Montreal, Canada and got to meet a bunch of the top comedians in the world. In this photo, he has just won a game of ball hockey in a match that was Comedians versus Industry.

A view from a special house that was a dream-come-true to several people.

A view of downtown Boston on a fine fall day in 2018 when close ally, Jim, came to visit and see the sights of New England.

Vermont in the fall in 2018.

A big rock at Kaanapali, Hawaii that the author jumped off a few times in 2011.

A rusted-out car on the road to Hana.

A special beach on Maui.

A waterfall that delighted thr author on Maui.

The greens and blues of this picture taken on Maui blew the author
away in 2011.

The author in his youth on Maui.